CYBERSECURITY IN THE
AGE OF AI

A Practitioner's Guide to Leveraging AI for Enhanced Security

Dr. Felix Hernandez

(CISSP, CISM, CCSP, CDPSE, PMP, CEH)

Legal & Disclaimer

The content and information in this book are consistent and truthful, and they have been provided for informational, educational, and business purposes only.

The content and information in this book have been compiled from reliable sources, which are accurate based on the author's knowledge, belief, expertise, and information. The author cannot be held liable for any omissions and errors.

Content

CHAPTER ONE

Introduction

One would think that artificial intelligence (AI) and cybersecurity are like oil and water, which may never mix well. However, in today's digital era, the reverse is true, as we can spot AI and cybersecurity working together. This represents an incredible advancement for the digital space.

While AI retains its ability to learn, recognize patterns, and predict outcomes, cybersecurity depends on human expertise and fixed rules to spot and stop threats to data and online security. It would seem that AI might be used to undermine data and online security systems. Still, there are several scenarios where both AI and cybersecurity take the stage collaboratively, acting towards the same goal.

For example, AI algorithms can sort through large amounts of data to identify mistakes and anomalies that might elude human notice. Unfortunately, cybercriminals equally exploit the same AI technologies for more sophisticated attacks. A clear example is how IBM's X-Force Red team proved that AI is capable of crafting convincing phishing emails and fooling 70% more people than those crafted by human beings. Amazing, isn't it? Well, it means that we need to understand the interplay of AI and cybersecurity better in order to find better ways to harness the benefits in relation to cybersecurity while preventing its misuse.

Importance and Relevance of AI

It is super important to prioritize cybersecurity in today's highly connected world. The widespread use of Internet of Things (IoT) devices, the increase in remote workers, and the reliance on cloud services create more opportunities for cyber threats. Gartner predicts that by 2025, there will be 75 billion connected devices worldwide, each one risking being a target for possible cyberattacks.

Even today, cyber-attacks are becoming more sophisticated as attackers get more creative with advanced methods to sneak past online defenses. This is where AI comes in handy to support our efforts as human beings. With AI, human analysts can improve how quickly and effectively they respond to threats, making it a worthy tool in today's cybersecurity toolbox.

Understanding how AI and cybersecurity work together is vital for protecting cyberspace. This book provides an in-depth exploration of this relationship by showcasing the latest trends, challenges, and future directions in the field.

In this book, we will explore how AI is transforming cybersecurity. We will take you through the topics one step at a time, beginning with the basic concepts and moving on to advanced applications, the latest trends, and expert opinions.

In the next chapter, you'll learn about the fundamentals of AI and cybersecurity, including basic concepts. Later chapters will dive into more specifics about AI applications in cybersecurity. Real-life case studies and instances will show you how these technologies work in practice.

The book will also discuss the ethical and regulatory issues related to using AI in cybersecurity. By the end, you'll have a detailed understanding of the challenges and opportunities AI brings to cybersecurity, giving you the knowledge to navigate this complex field effectively.

CHAPTER TWO

Fundamentals of AI and Cybersecurity

The first step to learning the fundamentals of artificial intelligence (AI) and cybersecurity is to appreciate them as separate subjects. Afterward, you can proceed to find their linkage and interaction. AI includes many subfields that contribute to its broader capabilities.

The subfields below make up the key concepts, and we shall discuss them briefly, one after the other, in this chapter.

Machine Learning, Neural Networks, Deep Learning, Generative AI

Machine learning (ML) is a core component of AI, enabling algorithms to learn from data to make predictions or decisions without being programmed end-to-end.

The human brain inspires **neural networks** by design and functionality. They are made up of layers of nodes that process input data and produce outputs or results.

Deep learning is a subset of ML and makes use of large neural networks with many layers. This is the reason for the "deep," showing the ability to handle complex patterns and large datasets. This approach has brought about some drastic changes and inclusions, such as image and speech recognition.

Generative AI is a newer branch involving AI models that can create new content. For instance, Generative Adversarial Networks (GANs) can produce realistic images and videos. OpenAI's GPT-4, a large language model, demonstrates generative AI's capabilities by producing human-like body of text and images, based on given prompts. A 2023 report showed that AI's ability to generate content independently has sparked both excitement and concern, particularly regarding its use in creating deep fakes or automating tasks traditionally performed by human beings.

Evolution and Advancements in AI

Human beings began the journey of exploring AI in the mid-20th century. We have pioneers like Alan Turing and John McCarthy laying the groundwork for modern AI as we know it. The early AI systems depended on rules and did not have the flexibility of modern models. Let's see the evolution of AI, categorized into several phases below:

1. **Symbolic AI Between the 1950s and 1980s:** The early AI systems depended on symbolic reasoning, where rules and logic were responsible for producing outcomes. The problem with this approach was its challenge with complex, real-world situations.

2. **Statistical AI Between 1990 and 2000:** The gradual development of statistical methods also increased the computational power of these systems. This led to the rise of machine learning, where algorithms could learn from the data you input to improve their performance over time.

3. **The present Deep Learning Era of 2010 and counting:** Deep learning came about through the availability of big data and powerful GPUs. Now, breakthroughs like AlexNet (2012) in image recognition showcase deep learning potential.

One of the most remarkable advancements is the transformer models, which have natural language processing as their strong suit. BERT (2018) and GPT-3 (2020) showed significant language learning, understanding, and generation abilities. Suffice it to say that the rapid evolution of AI continues to shape industries. What's more, there are also more predictions indicating that the AI market could contribute 826.73 billion US dollars by 2030.

Below is the chart depicting the worldwide AI market size from 2020 to 2030 in billion U.S. dollars.

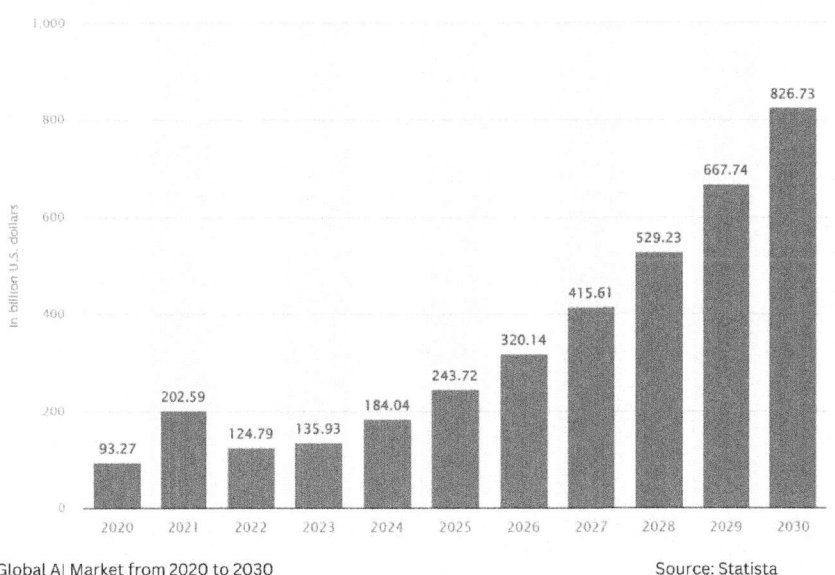

Global AI Market from 2020 to 2030   Source: Statista

Real-World Applications of AI Beyond Cybersecurity

The application of AI in the real world goes beyond its involvement in cybersecurity. In fact, AI is actively transforming various sectors in the real world, such as healthcare, finance, and even entertainment.

In healthcare, AI has advanced medical diagnostics and predictive analytics to enhance patients' care. For example, Google's DeepMind developed an AI model capable of detecting over 50 eye diseases from retinal scans with an accuracy matching that of expert ophthalmologists. Nowadays, AI-powered robots have improved the processes involved in generating diagnostic results, reducing errors.

In finance, AI algorithms play a pivotal role in analyzing market trends, detecting fraudulent activities, and optimizing trading strategies. A clear case is seen in how JPMorgan Chase's COiN platform uses Artificial Intelligence to review legal documents[5], saving an estimated 360,000 hours of annual work.

Also, self-driving cars like Tesla's Autopilot and optimized logistics lend credence to AI's benefits in the transportation sector.

AI also makes entertainment and media better with the advent of recommendation systems like Netflix's algorithms that suggest content based on user preferences. We can also see more real-world applications of AI in agriculture. These ensure precision farming techniques to optimize crop yields.

From all indications, the applications of AI in the real world are vast, reaching beyond cybersecurity and cutting across several unimaginable fields.

Understanding Cybersecurity

The basis of cybersecurity rests on the CIA Triad: *Confidentiality, Integrity, and Availability*. These core principles are responsible for the development and implementation of safety measures geared toward protecting information systems.

1. Confidentiality makes sensitive information accessible only to authorized persons. This quality is enhanced by techniques like encryption, access controls, and data masking to safeguard information from unauthorized access. The end-to-end encryption in messaging apps like WhatsApp, for instance, ensures that only you and the person with whom you are communicating can read the messages, protecting your conversation from eavesdroppers.

2. Integrity maintains the accuracy and reliability of data, making sure that information is not available for unauthorized handling or alteration. Techniques like checksums, digital signatures, and hashing are excellent tools for verifying data integrity. Incidentally, the Blockchain technology used in cryptocurrencies like Bitcoin provides a decentralized method for ensuring transaction integrity. This makes it nearly impossible to influence transaction records once validated unduly.

3. Availability makes sure that information and resources are accessible when you need them. It is important to know that

8

measures like regular backups ensure that your systems continue to function optimally, even during unforeseen disruptions. For instance, cloud service providers like Amazon Web Services (AWS) make use of distributed data centers to ensure high availability and resilience in the fight against data loss or downtime.

Common Threats: Malware, Phishing, Ransomware, Zero-Day Exploits

Cybersecurity is an endeavor and a concept that is not immune to attacks. In fact, the protective nature of cybersecurity exposes it to potential threats seeking to exploit any vulnerabilities in systems and networks. It's more about attacking your data defenses. Now, let's consider them in detail to discover how they operate and what measures we can take against them.

- Malware: They are malicious software like viruses, worms, and trojans created to damage, disrupt, or gain unauthorized access to computer systems. A typical example is seen in the WannaCry ransomware attack in 2017 that infected over 230,000 computers in 150 countries, encrypting files and also asking for ransom payments in Bitcoin.

- Phishing attacks: These are often fraudulent communications, usually in the form of emails, that appear to come from reputable sources or companies. The goal is to trick recipients into revealing sensitive information about themselves, companies, or projects. In 2020, Google reported blocking 18 million COVID-19-related phishing emails daily.

- Ransomware is a type of malware that manifests as phishing attacks in the sense that it encrypts a victim's data while the attackers demand payment for the decryption key. A clear example of a phishing attack and malware is the Colonial Pipeline attack in 2021, which resulted in significant fuel supply disruptions in the U.S.

- Zero-day exploits: These types of attacks target previously unknown vulnerabilities in software, such that there is no time for developers to issue patches. For instance, the Stuxnet worm, discovered in 2010, exploited zero-day vulnerabilities to target Iran's nuclear facilities. This demonstrated the potential for state-sponsored cyber warfare. You can see that having a good understanding of these threats is critical for developing effective cybersecurity strategies and protecting digital assets.

Cybersecurity Strategies and Frameworks

Cyber threats need proper handling to prevent further damage. As a result, organizations adopt various cybersecurity strategies and frameworks. We will consider a few in this piece as follows:

- The Defense-in-Depth Approach: This strategy works by layering multiple security measures to protect against a wide range of cybersecurity threats. Examples include but are not limited to firewalls, intrusion-detection systems, and antivirus software. These measures create a multi-faceted defense system for their users.

- The NIST Cybersecurity Framework: This measure, developed by the National Institute of Standards and Technology, provides a comprehensive guide for managing and reducing cybersecurity risks. It is made up of five core functions: **Identify, Protect, Detect, Respond, and Recover.** This framework helps you assess your cybersecurity posture and implement effective security practices.

- ISO/IEC 27001: It is an international standard for information security management systems (ISMS). It provides a systematic approach to managing sensitive company information to ensure it remains safe. If you observe compliance with ISO/IEC 27001, it demonstrates a commitment to cybersecurity, thus enhancing trust with stakeholders and customers.

- Zero Trust Architecture: This strategy assumes that threats can exist both within and outside the network. It requires strict verification for any user or device attempting to access resources, minimizing the risk of unauthorized access. An excellent example is Google's BeyondCorp initiative, allowing employees to work securely from any location without relying on traditional VPNs.

So, there you have it! By integrating these strategies and frameworks, you can build robust cybersecurity defenses for yourself and your organization, ensuring the protection of their digital assets regardless of the massive attacks on cybersecurity.

CHAPTER THREE

How AI is Transforming the Threat Landscape

Over the years, the threat landscapes have evolved across industries, from public health to physical, economic, and geopolitical security. The rise of AI has introduced new threats that did not exist years back. As technology evolves, so does the threat landscape. Also, there are unique differences between the technology threat landscape and the cybersecurity threat landscape, as can be seen in the table below:

	Cybersecurity Threat Landscape	Technology Threat Landscape
Primary Focus	Security of digital information and IT infrastructure.	Risks associated with emerging technologies across various fields.
Types of Threats	Malware, phishing, ransomware, data breaches, DDoS attacks.	Misuse of AI, ethical concerns of biotech, robotics safety, deepfakes.
Main Concerns	Data privacy, network security, and information integrity.	Ethical use of technology, unintended consequences, long-term effects.
Affected Entities	Businesses, governments, and individuals rely on digital technologies.	Wider society, including industries leveraging emerging tech public policy domains.
Mitigation Strategies	Firewalls, antivirus software, security protocols, and cybersecurity awareness training.	Ethical guidelines, regulatory frameworks, public awareness, research on long-term impacts.

In this chapter, I will be focusing on the cybersecurity threat landscape.

AI-Powered Attacks

So, what comes to your mind when you hear AI-powered attacks? To simplify what that means, it is a kind of cyber threat that uses artificial intelligence and natural processing languages to fool and or compromise critical systems or endpoints of organizations or steal sensitive information. Malicious hackers often use AI-generated text, phishing emails, and elements of social engineering to breach standard security protocols. The scale and scope of these attacks are becoming more complex by the day. AI can threaten actors and trick people into giving out their treasured personal details to allow for dubious activities. These AI-powered attacks are possible due to the ability of the AI to manipulate machine learning (ML) and language models to create personalized phishing emails. It makes it very difficult to tell otherwise. AI can learn and generate emails that sound humanlike from the massive pool of available data and human intelligence, creating convincing emails that are almost impossible to differentiate from human-written without too many grammar issues using authentic language styles. This is to fool individuals and trick them into handing over their personal and sensitive data.

These attacks are a big challenge, even for cybersecurity professionals and teams. It would be right to say that AI-based tools have increased the scope of cybersecurity attacks and made it more challenging to track threat signs and avoid such attacks. In adversarial attacks, AI-generated content is most often used to trick systems that compromise security standards, putting national security assets on the brink of attacks.

Mechanisms of AI-driven cyber threats: Automated attacks, AI-generated phishing, deep fakes

The National Association of State Chief Information Officers issued calls to corporate IT leaders and the government in March 2024 about existing security challenges that have taken new dimensions in their threat levels.

Currently, cybersecurity awareness training has become a priority for most governments in their bid to stem these recurring threats.

Modern AI-powered phishing attacks in the form of text, audio messages, videos, and emails continue to target government organizations at an unprecedented scale. This form continues to pose severe challenges to professional cybersecurity experts due to their almost impossible detectable signs like formatting errors, typos, and various mistakes often associated with previously targeted spear-phishing and phishing campaigns. Before the emergence of Generative AI like GPT, you could detect phishing emails by spotting typos and formatting errors; hackers now use Generative AI to step up their game by writing error-free phishing content.

Another troubling aspect is AI-powered deep fakes, which can accurately mimic a human or an individual's voice, face, and gestures. The new kinds of attack tools available today are capable of delivering fraudulent messages and disinformation at larger and more sophisticated levels than ever before.

There is news about fake messages mimicking President Biden, Florida Gov. Ron DeSantis, and many CEOs in the private sector. Other than its political impact and elections, we've seen instances of deep fakes where a video of a multinational company CFO tricked staff into making bank transfers that led to the loss of over $ 20 million.

Knowing the dangers before us, how can businesses deal with these new data threats? The discourse surrounding cybersecurity awareness training is evolving, with a growing emphasis on pushing beyond traditional methods to adopt more comprehensive and all-encompassing strategies. These enhanced measures are crucial for effectively countering the ever-evolving cyber threats faced by individuals and businesses alike.

I have had the privilege of leading initiatives at this advanced level, witnessing firsthand the remarkable results that such an approach can achieve.

To have robust and effective security awareness training, there must be a change in security culture. It should be such that everyone is responsible, asks questions about things they are confused about, reports risks, and understands that security goes beyond the workplace and everything about their personal and family security.

With all said, now how does one quickly and effectively deal with AI-generated attacks?

The first way to deal with these is by giving employees the proper training to detect these modern and highly sophisticated phishing attacks. They should have the appropriate knowledge to identify the authenticity of the content and sources received, such as:

- Irregular pattern in audio and video quality
- Voice synchronization or lip sync mismatch
- Unrealistic facial expressions
- Improved detection skills
- Using watermarks to customize videos and images
- Unrealistic speech or behavior pattern

Secondly, provide your employees with the necessary tools and teach them techniques and processes to verify authentic messages. With these tools in place, you can now design and develop a process whereby employees can question the authenticity of a message by making it go through various authentication processes purposely designed by the management team. Also, they should be empowered to report any deep fake content as they identify it.

The third is that you need to incorporate or bring on board new enterprise tools that use AI to figure out if a message is fraudulent or not. In just the same way iron sharpens iron, we also need AI to deal with it. Therefore, by using AI-powered modern enterprise tools, you can counter AI-generated spam messages in a similar way that email security tools identify and prevent traditional phishing links and spam suspicion messages. There are even more sophisticated tools that allow employees to check for fraudulent messages or images when automatically set up for all incoming emails.

So far, we have come to understand that cyber-attacks use deep fakes to fool humans, and this is fast eroding trust in the digital space.

Case studies of notable AI-powered attacks (e.g., AI-enhanced ransomware, spear phishing)

Since the dawn of 2023, generative AI and artificial intelligence dominated the news, and they are fast taking over when it comes to ransomware attacks. For instance, AI can enhance phishing attacks and access networks and automated systems powered by AI for further reach. For more than a year now, this format has driven ransomware to new levels and heights, and still, the level of these attacks continues to pitch even higher without a sign of a plateau any time soon. Even with the success recorded so far in dealing with traditional attack methods in 2023 and beyond, attackers would now turn to AI to generate more effective attacks.

The research analyzed 175 cases of ransomware attacks successfully carried out worldwide and reported between August 2022 and July 2023. The researchers categorized and tracked healthcare, education, and municipalities under primary categories. After the research, the number of reported attacks doubled, and it has been observed to increase yearly.

The level of attacks on sectors varies. Industries concerned with infrastructure have lower volumes of attacks compared to sectors such as healthcare, education, and municipalities. However, the number of attacks on infrastructure-based industries increased in subsequent years by twice the amount of the previous year. Education sectors and municipalities continued to be soft targets due to limited resources to enhance security in their cyberspaces. Attacks on healthcare and infrastructure can immensely impact people's lives; attackers know this and try to exploit it to increase their chances of being paid. Several countries across the world have made it mandatory to report cyber security incidents in one or more of these sectors.

The frequency of ransomware attacks continues to rise year after year throughout the five industries mentioned in the previous paragraphs. The financial sector has so far been successful in warding off most attacks and seems to be the only sector that has been able to achieve this level of success. The range of the attacks on healthcare went up from 12% to 18%. It increased from 12% to 21% for municipalities and from 5% to 18% for education, while it went up from 8% to 10% for infrastructure. Similarly, reports on attacks on the financial industry dropped from 6% to 1%, proving that the financial sector is doing well in protecting its system. Also, the volumes of ransomware attacks on sectors other than the previously mentioned show the same increasing pattern, even though attacks were least reported in these sectors.

The frequency of ransomware attacks, specifically on software businesses, has increased. Most businesses use software, making them vulnerable to software supply chain attacks, which have become rampant forms of attacks on the media, manufacturing, and retail sectors.

Impact on critical industries: Healthcare, education, local governments

The AI revolution has brought tremendous improvements to various sectors by enhancing efficiencies and offering cutting-edge solutions to problems that seemed to defy solutions before the advent of AI. Despite the numerous benefits of artificial intelligence, it also comes with various levels of threats, as we have seen in the paragraphs above. Critical sectors such as education, local government, and health are constantly under cyber-attacks, bringing about severe consequences.

Healthcare

The healthcare sector is at the top of most attackers' priority lists. Healthcare systems manage important and sensitive patient data that are essential for the patient's well-being, making them all the more attractive to cyber attackers who are hungry for these sensitive data. Malicious hackers can use AI to carry out extensive and sophisticated attacks on hospital systems that could lead to a data breach with devastating outcomes.

The Universal Health Service attack in 2020 was a typical example of the impact of AI threat on the healthcare sector. The ransomware attack led to far-reaching system downtime, which caused a whopping $ 67 million to be lost to hackers.

Attackers can use AI to identify and exploit vulnerabilities within systems at an accelerated pace, which can compromise patients' records and disrupt patients' care. The resultant effects can be far worse than life-threatening as it could lead to delayed treatments and risk the overall efficiency of the care of a patient.

Unfortunately, the healthcare sector, particularly hospitals, lacks the sophisticated cybersecurity governance necessary to ward off these advanced threat levels, making them vulnerable to data breaches and financial consequences. Still, we need AI to counter these threats, so it is necessary to integrate AI into healthcare cybersecurity to protect sensitive patients' data.

Education
Everyday education is becoming more reliant on technology for improved learning and administration, which makes it a lucrative target for AI-generated attacks. Learning institutions keep a massive volume of data on staff and students, which makes data breaches in the education sector a significant concern.

Clark County School District attack of 2021 is a notable example of a ransomware attack on the education sector. Employees' and students' information was exposed during this attack, which caused disruptions. The levels of these attacks are aggravated by AI, which causes frequent and damaging consequences. The resultant effects of these breaches are disruptions in the learning process. That means schools may suffer extensive downtime, affecting the student's education.

There are also financial costs to these attacks, whereby institutions are often forced to pay ransom or even upgrade security measures.

Local Government

Governments take care of essential responsibilities and make the environment conducive for thriving businesses and people. However, local government manages such responsibilities at the local level, such as the management of essential services such as electricity, water supplies, and emergencies, which makes it an attractive spot for hackers. An AI-powered cyber-attack on local government can have impactful effects, which could disrupt public service deliveries, causing widespread chaos.

A typical local government attack was the ransomware attack by cyber attackers in Baltimore in 2019. Public services were paralyzed during this attack, and it cost the city more than $ 18 million to restore them, as well as the revenue losses that followed. The lack of technical know-how for local governments to deal with these kinds of problems makes them all the more vulnerable.

An AI-powered attack disrupts daily life, affecting public services like transportation. The economic consequences can be significant, as more financial resources would be needed to restore essential services and improve security generally.

As AI-powered attacks evolve, businesses need to invest in employees' awareness and training and make it an ongoing affair. The employees are the first line of defense when it comes to cybersecurity. Investing in your people will not only secure your critical infrastructure but also guarantee that you comply with different regulations such as GDPR, HIPAA, and others. In the next chapter, I will dwell more on how you can adopt a proactive approach to establishing AI-powered cybersecurity measures.

CHAPTER FOUR

AI in Cyber Defense

AI is fast finding its way into the defense of our cyberspace. However, AI can power threats and compromise cybersecurity. But remember, in Chapter 3, we made it clear that it can be used equally to counter threats. AI is a double-edged sword, and the priority depends on what side we are using. In this chapter, our focus will be on "AI in Cyber Defense." You can figure out what we are talking about when we talk defense. If not, then this is it; it is simply protection against potential threats and all the processes involved in arriving at that protection.

Additionally, defense could mean removing a threat after it seems to have been incurred in a way that is not wanted. With all that said, cyber defense provides protection or removes threats from our system or cyberspace and that can be achieved using AI.

With AI, you can analyze, monitor, detect, and respond to threats that may have occurred in your cyberspace quickly and immediately as they occur. AI can analyze incredibly massive datasets to pick up recurring patterns that may tell the presence of a threat. It can run scans through an entire network to detect any loopholes or weaknesses that can be exploited to prevent any such attack with that pattern and even more.

AI can detect these threats by monitoring and analyzing behavioral patterns within the system network. It then uses such patterns to develop a baseline that allows it to pick up abnormal behaviors and limit or even stop unauthorized access to the rest of the system. This way, it helps to prioritize risks, probe for any malware possibility, and detect intrusions before they can cause harm.

Adequate implementation of AI in cyber defense brings automation to cybersecurity, removing a chunk of expendable resources and saving plenty of time that usually comes with repetitive tasks. It also means that human hands are removed, limiting the chances of human errors.

AI-Based Threat Detection and Response

Let's begin with the question, "How can AI-based threats be detected, and what possible response could follow?" To answer such a question, you first need to understand how these threats are detected and undergo a short series of processes, and they are as follows:

1. **Data Collection and Analysis:**
- Log Aggregation: The process begins by collecting data from various sources, such as system logs, user behavior, and network traffic.
- Behavior analysis: After collecting a substantial amount of data, the AI uses algorithms to build a normal behavior baseline and detect any abnormal behavior that may be indicative of a threat.

2. **Threat detection:**
- Signature-based detection: AI uncovers all threats that are of a similar pattern as the established baseline
- Anomaly detection: any abnormal behavior is then flagged as a threat.
- Threat intelligence integration: AI uses external threat intelligence feeds to stay up to date with trends, attack vectors, and patterns.

3. **Automated Response:**
- Incidence response blueprint: Here, all response actions are outlined and automatically executed according to the type and sophistication of the threat detected.
- Mitigation and Containment: The AI now quarantines all affected files and systems or even blocks dubious IPs before applying patches to the vulnerable ends.
- Remediation: Finally, it restores the affected system to normal and removes all threats.

4. Constant Learning and Improvement:

- Machine learning models: AI's machine learning capabilities allow it to train itself on new data to improve its detection accuracy and reduce the number of false responses.

- Feedback loops: The AI fortifies systems further by incorporating feedback from security analysts to improve its response strategies.

Applications in threat detection: Anomaly detection, predictive analytics.

Applications in threat detection include the use of AI technologies to identify, analyze, and mitigate any potential threat lurking in an organization's IT landscape. That is, the applications rely on the capabilities of AI to boost traditional security measures. Thereby making them more effective and efficient in identifying threats and responding to them accordingly. Applications in threat detection involve:

- Anomaly detection: the AI scans and monitors your systems and network to pick up any abnormal behavior and patterns that seem to be off the norm. Its machine learning capabilities allow it to learn from established data and continue to adjust to new types of anomalies, which improves the system. Then, a Generative AI helps create what we call synthetic anomalies to enhance its detective models, thereby making the system resilient against new threats. Unusual login and zero-day attacks might be detachable under anomaly detection.

- Predictive analytics: AI then attempts to predict future threat patterns by analyzing historical data that shows previous threat patterns. With its machine learning, it can study massive datasets and identify sophisticated patterns. Also, Gen AI adds to its predictable Analysis, still using history and even false data to simulate new attacks in the future. It is helpful in predicting threat vectors and keeping up with trends and attack patterns.

- Behavioral analytics: unlike predictive analytics, it is more focused on user behavior to detect or identify threats. Sometimes, standard security protocols may not detect or fish out potential threats, especially when brilliantly fixed as part of a standard procedure. AI can pick up this threat by identifying unusual user behavior. Still, it uses its machine learning capabilities to automate the Analysis of data anomalies that are indicative of a threat. Such anomalies should be noticed in the manual review process. Now, Generative AI models those abnormal and normal behaviors to improve its analysis, which allows systems to detect and identify compromised accounts and insider threats better.

- Pattern recognition: Here, AI can identify repeated patterns or data structures, which allows it to detect and categorize established forms of cybersecurity threats. The AI's machine learning capabilities will enable it to automate this identification process, enhancing recognition accuracy. Generative AI has developed a new template for attack pattern simulations to improve its learning capabilities. With pattern recognition, your system can identify

24

threat actors' relationships, recognize spear-phishing campaigns, and classify malware.

Incident response and mitigation strategies using AI

Having a proactive strategy for your system or network security management should be a part of your approach to dealing with any threat. It allows you and your systems to respond to breach incidences quickly and prevent them while reducing the impact such threats may cause.

Incident response is critical in any organization's security posture as it represents the first line of defense during an attack, and with an AI defense, it learns the pattern of this threat and develops a better risk mitigation approach against new threats. When you automate incidence response with an AI, you empower your systems to deal with threat incidents efficiently at a more incredible speed and with less effort required from team members. This minimizes human errors and enables you to deal with threats in real time. An AI achieves a successful incidence response through the following:

- **Automated Incident Response:** When AI is allowed to handle your systems' incident response, it automates your routine incident response tasks by isolating infected devices, updating firewall rules, and blocking dubious IP addresses. AI automation identifies and resolves threats faster with minimal human errors.

- **Contextual Analysis:** Here, the AI provides a comprehensive analysis of your security incidents through data correlation from different sources. Such information allows the security teams to grasp the impact and scope of the incident, which may trigger more effective response strategies.

- **Decision Support:** AI is useful for security analysts as it provides recommendations based on similar previous work. This helps us make well-informed decisions in a timely manner, which really improves response efficiency.

Now, AI Mitigation Strategies include:

- **Continuous Monitoring:** AI monitors your systems and network to find abnormal patterns.
- **Dynamic Defense Mechanism:** It allows for a dynamic Defense such as real-time threat hunting and adaptive authentication.
- **Post-Incident Analysis:** When all incidents are resolved, the AI assists in running post-Incident Analysis, which can help analysts get a clearer picture of the core problem.

Real-world applications

So far, there has been tremendous recognition and application of AI in various industries. Cybersecurity has, to a fair extent, benefited from AI. Research shows that about 34% of organizations will incorporate generative AI in the coming years. You may have come across various online articles about AI's impracticality in the real world. Do not let that discourage you because I will show real-world examples of organizations that have successfully implemented AI in their cybersecurity practices.

- **Web Application (BurpGPT):** BurpGPT is a Burp suite extension that incorporates the Open AI GPT model to carry out extensive scans passively to identify customized vulnerabilities. Users can run all sorts of traffic-based Analysis, which improves the chances of finding vulnerabilities that traditional scanning models easily miss.

- **Workflow Automation (Blink):** Many organizations need help to automate simple and routine tasks due to rigid SOAR tool requirements or the need for technical skills to code various steps. Thanks to AI, these tasks have become more simplified through the generation of new automated workflows.

A Typical example of a tool that simplifies the building of workflows is *Blink Copilot*, which leverages generative AI. It takes a chunk of the burden from you having to understand each integration in order to develop sophisticated automation. Blink helps teams expand what they should automate, such as compliance check device management and syncing I AM roles.

- *Vulnerability Prioritization (EPSS):* The Exploit Prediction Scoring System(EPSS) is another AI-powered tool that can help organizations predict the chances of potentially existing vulnerabilities being actively exploited. This tool came about due to collaboration between organizations and researchers. The EPSS uses machine learning algorithms to generate scores pointing to probable exploitation.

- *Security OPs (Virus Total Code Insight):* Virus Total Code Insight is another area where AI is making a tremendous impact on security operations. It helps analyze suspicious files and URLs. It is a new AI-powered tool, and a Google subsidiary introduced code insights and uses Google Cloud Security AI Workbench to analyze code behaviors and semantics.

- *IAM Security Testing (Tenable EscalateGPT):* another real-world implementation success is the Identity Access and Management security testing using Tenable EscalateGPT. The Tenable EscalateGPT is an AI-powered tool that helps discover privilege escalation and opportunities in the AWS IAM configurations.

Certification and Complication of Security

Identifying security complications is a way of improving your cybersecurity posture against threats. Through fortification, you can:

- *Enhance Threat Detection:* AI can improve your system's ability to detect complex threats through machine learning capabilities, pattern recognition, and advanced analytics. It can also effectively identify sophisticated malware and zero-day vulnerabilities.

- *Proactive Defense:* AI allows for a real-time response to threats and keeps your system active against new threat patterns.

- *Automated Response:* AI security tools installed in your system can automate your system responses and identify threats, reducing the time required to react and mitigate risks quickly. Automated responses could include blocking malicious IPs, initiating incident response protocols, and isolating the affected system.

- *Comprehensive Monitoring:* Your system enjoys continuous monitoring of all system networks and their activities, user behaviors, and anomalies with AI.

- *Improve accuracy:* An AI's constant learning capabilities, such as machine learning, coupled with the absence of human efforts, allow it to reduce false positives and enhance the overall effectiveness and accuracy of threat detection and response capabilities.

- *Resource Optimization:* As AI takes away efforts from humans and automates processes, it allows for a more efficient use of time and human resources.

However, you need to be aware of security complications, including integration complexities, increased attack surfaces, dependency on data quality, model drift, ethical/legal challenges, operational costs, explainability, and trust.

AI as a Decision Assistant in Security Operations Centers (SOCs)

AI has brought more efficiency in all processes for Security Operations Centers(SOCs) through;

- Improved threat detection and Analysis
- Incident responses
- Data Management
- Enhancing SOC efficiency
- Continuous improvements; Reducing Fatigue for analysts
- Decision Support
- Future Trends

Automating Processes and Enhancing Security Measures

As we have discussed earlier in the chapter, AI can automate processes and, as a result, improve security. It automates processes such as:

- Routine Tasks
- Patch Management
- User Behavior Analytics

This automated task brings about enhanced security measures like:

- Advance Threat Detection
- Behavior Analysis
- Predictive Analysis

Challenges: API Hardening, Information Availability, AI Security Complexities

While AI significantly benefits Security Operations Centers (SOCs), it also presents several challenges that must be addressed to ensure effective and secure implementation.

API Hardening

- <u>Vulnerability Exposure:</u> When APIs are not properly secured, they can become a source of vulnerabilities. Most AI systems use multiple APIs to connect with data sources and security tools. Therefore, it is necessary to harden these APIs to ward off threats.

- <u>Authentication and Authorization:</u> To limit or control unauthorized access, you need strong authentication and Authorization mechanisms, such as multifactor authentication and OAuth.

- <u>Rate Limiting and Throttling:</u> allow for the maintenance of the reliability and availability of security tools, preventing API abuse and denial-of-services threats.

- <u>Input Validation:</u> This allows you to have a more stringent validation in place to avoid malicious and injection attacks that could compromise the security of the AI SOC and AI system.

Data Availability

- **Data Quality and Completeness:** AI is only as accurate as its provided data. That is, an AI needs complete and top-quality data to function efficiently.

- **Data integration:** After getting the quality and accurate data it needs, the AI can now integrate data from all the different sources to ensure the accuracy and reliability of your system.

- **Data Privacy and Compliance**: Managing sensitive data within regulatory frameworks (GDPR, CCPA, HIPAA) is always an arduous task. Therefore, AI systems must be able to deal with data safely while adhering to regulatory protocols.

- **Timely access:** Anything that would prevent an AI from accessing real-time data must be avoided to allow for more effective threat detection and response.

AI Security Complexities

- *Model Vulnerabilities:* models are often subject to attacks. Such attacks can be adversarial. That is why models must be protected against attacks.

- *Bias and Fairness:* Bias may be inherent in training models that AI can adopt, leading to faulty outcomes. Although ensuring that data are bias-free can be complex, it is a necessary task that must be accomplished.

- *Explainability:* AI systems can be black boxes with a non-transparent decision-making process, especially deep learning ones. A clearer interpretation and explanation of AI decisions are essential for accountability and trust issues.

- *Continuous Learning and Adaptation*: AIs can continuously learn and adapt to new threat landscapes. Another challenge is keeping hackers from tempering this learning capability.

- *Resource Intensive:* Advanced AI systems require significant computational power and infrastructure. Balancing these resource needs with other SOC operations is essential.

CHAPTER FIVE

AI Implementation Challenges for Cybersecurity

As the business world evolves, innovative technology such as Artificial intelligence is becoming a critical components of business operations. The ability to leverage the power of AI is separating forward-thinking companies from the rest. It is, therefore, imperative for businesses to figure out strategies for security, governance, and compliance when deploying AI technologies.

In this chapter, I will expound on the challenges this converge brings and how businesses can navigate them.

When deploying AI in cybersecurity, the first step is to assess your AI Cyber Readiness. It would be best if you grasped your organization's specific needs. This goes beyond identifying threats; it also involves knowing your existing infrastructure and how AI can improve your cyber defenses. Imagine you're setting up a fortress to protect your kingdom. You need to figure out the kind of attacks you're likely to face. Are you dealing with malware, insider threats, or phishing? Each of these threats demands unique strategies and AI tools. This fundamental step forms the basis that guides your entire deployment process.

Once you have gained a clear understanding of your needs, the next step is to consider the AI solutions that are available. It's like picking the right tool from a toolkit. Do you need deep learning models for advanced threat protection or machine learning models for anomaly detection? The choice of the right AI solution is important as it impacts everything from data collection to model training. And let's not forget the integration aspect. Imagine adding a powerful new engine to an old car; it has to fit seamlessly. Your AI solutions must blend well with your existing cybersecurity infrastructure, often requiring some fine-tuning and customization.

One of the most significant technical challenges in deploying AI is data quality. Data is the essence of the AI models. If you feed poor-quality data into your models, you'll generate poor results. It's like trying to build a house with substandard materials; the structure is bound to collapse. Collecting data is the first challenge. You will need a lot of it, and it has to come from different sources like user activity data, network traffic logs, and more. The more comprehensive the data, the better your AI model will perform. But collecting data is just the beginning. Once you have it, you need to clean it. This process involves isolating errors, inconsistencies, and noise, which is similar to sorting through a huge pile of documents to find the relevant ones. Finally, the data needs to be accurately labeled, especially for supervised learning models. Accurate labeling is significant because if your data is mislabeled, your model will learn incorrect patterns, leading to ineffective security measures.

Model accuracy is another major technical challenge. The effectiveness of your AI in detecting and mitigating threats depends on the accuracy of the models. Overfitting and underfitting are common issues here. Overfitting is like learning a map for a specific route and getting lost for deviating slightly. Underfitting, on the other hand, is knowing too little to explore any route effectively. Balancing this is very important. Additionally, identifying the most relevant features and picking the right algorithms are crucial steps. It's like picking the right ingredients for a recipe and then choosing the best cooking method to bring out the flavors. Improving model accuracy involves cross-validation, ensemble methods, and hyperparameter tuning, which combine multiple models to enhance performance.

Computational resources are another hurdle. AI models, particularly those using deep learning, require significant computational power. This involves ensuring you have adequate processing power, memory, and storage. It's like needing a powerful engine for a high-performance car. Managing the cost of these resources can be expensive, and you need to ensure the returns justify the investment. As your data volume and model complexity grow, your infrastructure must be scalable. Think of it as expanding a factory to meet increasing demand. You can leverage cloud computing resources for scalable and cost-effective computation. You will also need to invest in high-performance hardware and optimize your algorithms for efficiency to help you manage the demands effectively.

Ethical AI for cybersecurity

Bias in AI can lead to unfair outcomes, and this is a major concern. If the training data is biased, the model will be biased, too. This is like building a worldview on one-sided information. Sometimes, the design of the algorithm itself introduces bias, which can lead to biased outcomes. And the impact of AI decisions can disproportionately affect certain groups. To mitigate bias, it's essential to adopt fairness-aware algorithms, ensure diversity in training data, and conduct regular bias audits. Fairness and transparency are also crucial. Making AI decisions understandable is important for building trust. If users can't comprehend how decisions are made, they won't trust the system. Establishing clear responsibility for AI decisions and maintaining open communication with stakeholders helps build accountability and trust.

Compliance with regulatory frameworks is critical for AI deployment in cybersecurity. This ensures that your solutions are not only effective but also legal. Data privacy regulations like GDPR and CCPA impose stringent data privacy requirements. Compliance is non-negotiable to avoid legal repercussions. Adhering to industry-specific security standards provides guidelines that help in building secure systems. Navigating the legal implications of AI decisions is complex, and understanding these implications is crucial. Staying informed about regulatory changes, implementing comprehensive data protection measures, and seeking legal counsel to understand the implications of AI deployment are crucial steps.

Overcoming the challenges in deploying AI for cybersecurity requires strategic planning and execution. Implementing robust data management practices addresses data quality issues. Establishing data governance frameworks ensures data integrity and quality. Leveraging automated tools for data cleaning and preprocessing can significantly improve efficiency and accuracy. Regular monitoring of data quality helps identify and rectify issues promptly.

To improve model accuracy, using cross-validation techniques ensures that your models generalize well to new data. Optimizing hyperparameters can enhance model performance significantly. Combining multiple models can improve accuracy and robustness. Managing computational resources effectively involves leveraging cloud services for scalable and cost-effective computation. Efficient allocation of resources ensures that you don't overspend or underutilize your computational power. Optimizing algorithms to reduce computational demands helps manage costs and improve efficiency.

Addressing ethical challenges involves implementing techniques to detect and mitigate bias in AI models. Adopting practices that enhance transparency and explainability builds trust. Engaging with stakeholders helps in understanding their concerns and building trust. Navigating regulatory and compliance issues involves keeping abreast of regulatory changes and industry standards. Seeking legal advice helps in understanding compliance requirements and navigating complex legal landscapes. Implementing robust data protection measures safeguards privacy and security.

Deploying AI for cybersecurity is a challenging but rewarding endeavor. By focusing on data quality, model accuracy, computational resources, ethical considerations, and regulatory compliance, organizations can navigate these challenges effectively. With careful planning, strategic implementation, and continuous improvement, AI can significantly enhance cybersecurity defenses, making them more robust, efficient, and fair. This journey, though fraught with challenges, ultimately leads to a stronger, more resilient cybersecurity posture capable of withstanding the evolving threat landscape.

CHAPTER SIX

Future Trends in AI and Cybersecurity

Several groundbreaking innovations have impacted the tech world. In this chapter, we shall explore transformative technologies such as **quantum computing, blockchain, and the Internet of Things**. Each of these technologies presents new challenges for cybersecurity.

Quantum Computing: uses quantum mechanics principles to solve complex problems that classical computers cannot address efficiently. This technology is set to disrupt various fields, including energy use, drug research, financial modeling, and autonomous vehicle navigation. Major tech companies like IBM, Amazon, Microsoft, and Google are investing heavily in quantum computing, forecasting a market value of 8.6 billion dollars, according to Statista.

One significant quantum computing algorithm, Shor's algorithm, has the potential to break encryption systems that secure today's internet traffic. Although large-scale practical deployment is not expected until at least the 2030s, the implications for cybersecurity are obvious. A threat actor using such technology could decrypt sensitive information, threatening personal, financial, and national security data.

Blockchain technology, known for its decentralized nature, also faces cybersecurity threats. A notable example is the "51% attack," where an entity can gain majority control of a blockchain network's computation power. This enables them to manipulate transaction history, stop transactions, prevent validator rewards, and double-spend. Historical examples include attacks on Ethereum Classic, Vertcoin, and Bitcoin Gold, which led to substantial financial losses and eroded trust in the affected cryptocurrencies. The threat shows the need for formidable security measures to secure blockchain networks.

Internet of Things (IoT) connects billions of devices, enhancing functionalities across homes, industries, and cities. However, this interconnectedness comes with significant cybersecurity challenges. IoT devices often lack strong security protocols, making them vulnerable to hacking and hijacking. Threat actors usually recruit vulnerable IoT devices to join an army of botnets to access sensitive data, disrupt services, or cause physical harm if critical infrastructure is targeted. As IoT adoption grows, so the need to secure them becomes paramount.

Implications for Cybersecurity

The integration of these emerging technologies into various sectors and business processes demands a rethinking of cybersecurity strategies.

Quantum computing could render current encryption methods obsolete, prompting the need for quantum-resistant encryption or post-quantum cryptography. In 2022, NIST revealed the first group of encryption tools that can withstand threats from future quantum computers. These algorithms were integrated to form part of NIST's quantum-resistant cryptographic standard.

Blockchain's susceptibility to 51% attack requires the development of more secure consensus algorithms and protective measures against majority control. In 2024 alone, the crypto industry recorded over a hundred security exploits, and the Blockchain Security Standards Council(BSSC) is working assiduously to establish companion audit schemes and standards for the blockchain industry.

In the IoT space, AI-driven security systems can detect vulnerabilities, automate threat detection, and respond to incidents in real-time, thus providing cutting-edge protection against cyber threats.

Predictions and Future Directions

Experts from various cybersecurity domains have shared their predictions for the future of AI and cybersecurity. Here are some notable insights:

Sam Curry, Global Vice President and CISO of Zscaler, anticipates **an increase in AI-driven disinformation campaigns, particularly during election years. The internet's unregulated nature allows bad actors to use AI-generated fake news to manipulate public opinion and behavior, posing significant risks to societal stability.**

Margareta Petrovic and Dr. KPS Sandhu from Tata Consultancy Services (TCS) highlight **the dual-edged nature of generative AI. While it enhances the sophistication of cyberattacks, it also offers opportunities to strengthen cybersecurity. AI-driven solutions can automate security measures, improve compliance, and enhance reporting, thereby transforming enterprise security postures.**

Kevin O'Connor, Director of Threat Research at Adlumin, warns about **the increased use of commercially available AI systems in social engineering attacks. AI's ability to integrate with personal information from social media can enable attackers to craft highly targeted and convincing phishing campaigns.**

Michael Crandell, CEO of Bitwarden, **introduces the concept of "Shadow AI," where employees use AI tools without organizational oversight. This creates significant cybersecurity and data privacy risks. Companies must adopt Managed AI policies, educate teams on safe AI practices, and monitor AI tool usage to mitigate these risks.**

Josh Aaron, CEO of Aiden, **predicts a focus on AI red teaming and bug bounties to identify and address AI-specific vulnerabilities. This proactive approach involves using diverse teams to test AI systems comprehensively, ensuring robust defenses against sophisticated threats.**

Brian Roche, Chief Product Officer at Veracode, **discusses the arms race between AI-driven defense and AI-assisted offense. He emphasizes the need for organizations to embrace AI and machine learning to stay ahead of evolving cyber threats, with AI-powered security solutions offering advanced threat detection and response capabilities.**

Experts also **foresee the emergence of a "poly-crisis" from AI-based cyberattacks targeting IT, cloud containers, and Industrial Control Systems (ICS). This scenario threatens not only financial stability but also human lives through cascading effects. Automated cyber defense leveraging AI will be crucial in adapting to new attack models and mitigating these multifaceted threats.**

The Future of Generative AI in Cybersecurity

Generative AI is poised to play a transformative role in cybersecurity. It can enhance threat detection, automate incident response, and improve the overall security posture of organizations. As generative AI evolves, it will become an essential tool in countering advanced cyber threats, enabling real-time adaptation to new attack vectors and reducing the window of vulnerability.

Long-Term Trends: Democratization of AI, Increased Accessibility, Improved Efficiency

The long-term trends in AI and cybersecurity point towards the democratization of AI, making advanced AI tools and technologies accessible to a broader audience.

This increased accessibility will empower smaller organizations and individuals to leverage AI to enhance their cybersecurity defenses. Moreover, AI-driven solutions will continue to improve efficiency, offering more robust, automated, and scalable security measures. This will be essential in managing the growing complexity and volume of cyber threats, ensuring a safer digital future for all.

The future of AI and cybersecurity is both promising and challenging. As emerging technologies like quantum computing, blockchain, and IoT evolve, they bring new opportunities and risks. AI will play a pivotal role in addressing these challenges, driving innovation, and enhancing cybersecurity. By staying ahead of trends and embracing AI-driven solutions, organizations can build resilient defenses against the ever-evolving cyber threat landscape.

CHAPTER SEVEN

Case Studies and Real-world Applications of AI in Cybersecurity

It's no secret that technological progress empowers hackers and cyber attackers to cause more harm. This corroborates the ancient African saying, "*When the hunter learns to shoot without missing, the bird must learn to fly without perching.*" Boosting cybersecurity in one of the smartest eras known to us requires that we invest significant energy in understudying how other organizations have thrived as far as this topic is concerned.

There can be no better way to fully grasp the extent to which AI is applied in the age of cybersecurity without looking at case studies and real-world applications. This chapter is dedicated to a dive deeper than you can imagine into how some organizations are leveraging AI to boost cybersecurity, the challenges they face, and insights from industry leaders.

We shall base our studies and analysis on five organizations making the best of AI to protect themselves and their digital assets from the smart clutches of new-age cyber criminals. We shall be considering the five below:

1. Darktrace
2. IBM Security
3. Symantec
4. JPMorgan Chase
5. Microsoft

1. Darktrace

Darktrace leverages AI for better cybersecurity by concentrating on threat detection and analysis using machine learning. This area of expertise has allowed the 6-year-old company to thrive in terms of AI-driven cybersecurity solutions. Darktrace's technology uses machine learning and AI to detect and respond to cyber threats as they happen. Machine learning allows them to master and predict patterns through which more attacks might surface after each threat interception. Their technology, akin to the human brain in learning, is today described as an "immune system" for the digital world since it continuously learns and adapts to new threats, just like human antibodies against biological invaders.

2. IBM Security

IBM has a long history of data expertise and protection, especially against phishing emails and malware. It leverages its AI platform to enhance cybersecurity through formidable strategies that include enhanced threat intelligence and automated security processes. Their AI platform analyzes lots of data, including blogs, research papers, and other online content, to fish out emerging threats and then suggest appropriate countermeasures.

3. Symantec

Symantec also ranks among the organizations making waves in the application of AI in cybersecurity. Their AI-driven solutions include advanced threat detection and automated response capabilities. Symantec's

AI can identify complex attack patterns and predict future threats, enabling proactive defense strategies.

4. JPMorgan Chase

JPMorgan Chase is one of the world's largest financial institutions that uses AI to protect against fraud. Their system, known as COiN (Contract Intelligence), engages machine learning to look up and interpret legal and financial documents. This strategy has helped them reduce the risk of fraud and financial crimes by identifying suspicious transactions and patterns that would have otherwise gone unnoticed by human analysts.

5. Microsoft

Microsoft remains one of the most popular tech companies in the world and also one of the most attacked. As a result, they have integrated AI into their Azure Security Center. What this AI-driven platform does is monitor network activity, detect anomalies, and provide suggestions for mitigating any risks. Their AI also helps in automating routine security tasks to free up more time for human security analysts to focus on more complex problems.

Success Stories and Lessons Learned

Now that you know, some organizations are making the best of AI to protect themselves and their digital assets from cybercriminals. It's time to look at some success stories and a few valuable lessons we can pick from these organizations. These success stories aren't all there is but merely notable examples to spark your interest in the application of AI towards achieving better cyber security.

Darktrace successfully implemented its AI solutions to detect and identify an unusual data transfer for a global bank as an insider threat. This success was largely due to the AI's machine-learning ability, causing it to learn and adapt to normal network behavior. In other words, any contrary network behavior becomes an anomaly. Now that, more than ever, we are more concerned with tightening cyber security, the success of Darktrace here promotes the importance of continuous learning and adaptation in cybersecurity.

IBM Security has recorded several success stories, especially with Watson. One significant case involved a healthcare provider who was facing incessant phishing attacks. IBM security, through Watson's aid, analyzed several quantities of data and discovered patterns in the phishing attempts. From there, the organization was able to implement targeted defenses, thereby reducing the phishing attack rate by 70%. Again, AI proved to be valuable in recognizing patterns beyond human observation as a critical step in combating cybercrimes.

Symantec recorded significant success when it used its AI capabilities to turn off a ransomware attack on a multinational corporation. The success of AI was due to the early detection of ransomware by identifying and recognizing unusual file encryption patterns. Then, we will isolate the systems that were affected by the malware. As a result of this interception, the ransomware was no longer able to spread, thus minimizing further damage.

JPMorgan Chase's success story is immaterial without its COiN platform. They used AI to review millions of legal documents and identified so many fraudulent transactions. As a result, they were able to save millions of dollars. They have also been able to record significant success in detecting sophisticated fraud schemes that may otherwise go unnoticed. They succeeded because of the effectiveness of AI in handling repetitive, data-intensive tasks, enabling humans to take care of more strategic roles.

Microsoft successfully used AI to detect weird traffic patterns affecting a major e-commerce organization that would have led to a serious distributed denial-of-service (DDoS) attack. This victory was due to its AI-driven Azure Security Center, which automatically deployed countermeasures to protect the company's commercial services, keeping them intact.

Challenges Faced and How They Were Overcome

Our five-focus organizations recorded significant success with applying AI to cybersecurity frameworks. However, they and other organizations not mentioned in this study faced many challenges. It is, therefore, important to consider the challenges faced by these companies to arm yourself with a possible line of action should you be in a similar situation. Here's a sneak peek into some challenges and how they overcame them. Again, we will continue with our five focus companies.

In the beginning, Darktrace struggled with false positives, which was quite frustrating. By false positives, the AI flagged normal activities as threats. As a result, it became burdensome for the security teams to review these false positive alerts. The company overcame this challenge by enhancing its machine learning algorithms to enable them to better distinguish normal from abnormal activities. A feedback loop was initiated, where security analysts provided input, and it was used to improve the AI's accuracy over time.

IBM Security's challenge was data integration. As a company, they dealt with large amounts of data from different sources, sometimes needing to be more organized. They needed help integrating these data sources, particularly those in different formats, which was a major challenge. IBM overcame this problem by developing advanced data integration tools. They also entered into partnerships with data providers and invested heavily in data cleaning and preprocessing techniques. These steps enabled them to achieve and maintain data quality.

Symantec had problems with AI transparency, leading to skepticism of AI-driven recommendations, especially when faced with vague rationale. They overcame this huddle by developing explainable AI models to explain the decision-making process.

For JPMorgan Chase, the problem was with employees who feared that AI would take their jobs. One significant instance of this resistance was legal analysts feeling super threatened by the COiN platform. The bank overcame this challenge by sensitizing employees that AI was developed to augment rather than replace human roles. They highlighted the obvious AI benefits, such as multitasking and handling repetitive tasks, to create time for more strategic and fulfilling work.

Microsoft encountered challenges with scaling its AI solutions across its vast customer base. For instance, each customer has unique needs and environments, making it problematic to apply a one-size-fits-all solution. They overcame this by developing AI components that could be customized and fixed in different environments. They also provided further support and resources to allow customers to tailor the AI to their specific needs.

Insights from Industry Leaders and Experts

The five organizations we have analyzed so far are run by certain leaders who manage their affairs. While it is useful to understudy the organizational process from afar, it makes a significant mark to hear it directly from the industry leaders. The essence is to provide some form of encouragement to other industry leaders looking to implement AI in cyber security frameworks. This section will showcase deeper insights from our five-focus industry leaders and experts.

Darktrace's CEO Nicole Eagan emphasizes the need for AI to learn and adapt in her quote continuously, **"Cyber threats are constantly evolving. AI systems must evolve, too. The key is not just detecting threats but adapting to new ones in real-time."** Her insight highlights the dynamic nature of cybersecurity and how necessary it is for AI systems to remain agile.

The General Manager at IBM Security, Marc van Zadelhoff, emphasizes the importance of collaboration between AI and human analysts. Here is his statement, **"AI can handle the heavy lifting of data analysis, but human intuition and expertise are irreplaceable. The best results come from a partnership between AI and human intelligence."** Van Zadelhoff's perspective presents the fantastic relationship between AI and human analysts in achieving optimal cybersecurity outcomes. This way, humans need not fear to be replaced by AI but to scale up to using AI as a worthy tool.

The former CEO of Symantec, Greg Clark, talked about the importance of transparency in AI-driven decisions. He notes, **"For AI to be trusted, it must be transparent. Security teams need to understand why AI makes certain recommendations. This builds trust and ensures**

better decision-making." Clark believes the critical role of explainability in gaining acceptance for AI technologies cannot be overstated.

Lori Beer, CIO of JPMorgan Chase, talked about the human aspect of AI integration. She explained, **"AI should be seen as an enabler, not a threat. It's about augmenting human capabilities and making their work more impactful. Communication and education are key to easing fears and resistance."** From Beer's perspective, we can see that the Cruz of the matter is more about clear communication and education in fostering a positive attitude towards AI.

Microsoft's corporate Vice President for Cybersecurity Solutions, Ann Johnson, is more concerned about the need for flexibility in AI usage. She states, **"Every organization is unique. AI solutions must be adaptable to fit different environments and needs. Providing customizable and scalable AI components ensures broader adoption and effectiveness."** Johnson's insight highlights the value of flexibility and customization in AI solutions to create variety in adoption and usage.

There are many more industry experts to learn from, but for this book and this chapter, we have decided to stay within our five-focused organizations. There is so much to know and learn regarding the application and integration of AI in cyber security as an endeavor if you are to stay ahead of more advanced cyber crimes. Leveraging AI for enhanced security has no terminal effect, and you must be willing to keep up with the latest trends and advancements as far as this issue is concerned.

CONCLUSION

Will AI Replace Human Analysts?

I want to round off this book with a question that resonates with many people's fears: **Will AI replace human analysts?**

We have seen AI disrupting operations across vertical sectors, and it is unimaginably impacting the cybersecurity profession. This AI-enabled shift is redefining the roles and tasks of cybersecurity practitioners and unveiling skill sets and roles.

Several regions globally are addressing the growing skill gaps in cybersecurity by establishing guidelines for the profession.
In the U.S., the National Initiative for Cybersecurity Careers and Studies (NICE) Framework covers public, private, and academic sectors. It outlines seven key cybersecurity functions, 33 specialty areas, and 52 specific work roles. These roles include governance, design, operations, threat management, analysis, and investigation.

The National Initiative for Cybersecurity Education (NICE) Workforce Framework

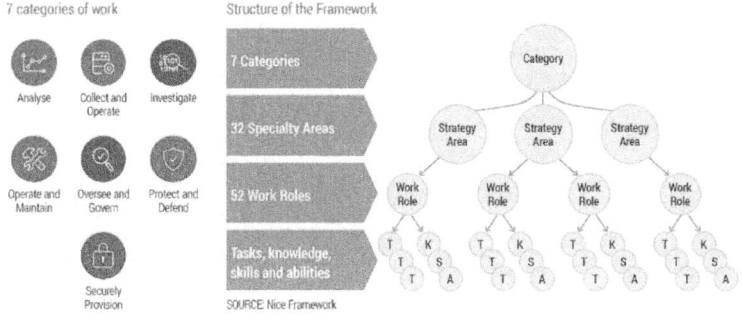

Europe's European Cybersecurity Skills Framework (ECSC) identifies 12 professional role profiles, including titles, tasks, skills, missions, knowledge, and competencies across legal, managerial, risk management, and operational roles. The U.K. CyberSecurity Council defines 16 specialisms in both technical and managerial fields, linking them to industry credentials to aid skill development.

These initiatives are vital due to the complexity introduced by AI and other transformative technologies. A holistic skill set is crucial for effective cybersecurity, emphasizing the need for professionals to understand the expanding business context and adjacent domains, such as risk, digital governance, and audit.
Additionally, understanding emerging technologies, such as AI, is essential for identifying risks, building controls, and implementing forensics and investigations in AI-enabled ecosystems.

The impact of AI on cybersecurity is transformative. Companies like IBM are already showcasing the potential of AI by automating incident responses, which accelerates alert investigations and triage by an average of 55%. This not only simplifies access for verified users but also reduces the cost of fraud by up to 90%. Microsoft, on the other hand, leverages AI to provide critical guidance to cybersecurity teams, enabling swift responses to incidents via Microsoft Copilot.

Given the current trajectory, it's evident that AI will significantly augment if not entirely replace, manual tasks in cybersecurity. Areas such as data collection, analytics, risk assessment, audits, cybersecurity operations, and even the design of cybersecurity architectures will increasingly rely on AI-driven solutions.

As we stand at the crossroads of this AI-driven transformation, organizations must adapt and integrate these advanced technologies into their cybersecurity strategies. Embracing AI enhances security measures, drives efficiency, and reduces costs, positioning businesses to tackle the complex threats of the digital age better.

If you're looking to navigate this evolving landscape with confidence, consider partnering with a seasoned consultant who brings over twenty-five years of experience in Information Technology, Information Security, Project Management, and Business Development. Growing up in the South Bronx, NYC, I learned the value of hard work and determination early on, propelling my professional journey to success.

I own and operate All American Technology Solutions Group, a leading consulting company providing IT services to small and medium-sized businesses. I also lead Strategic Sentinels, a boutique cybersecurity firm offering specialized services to non-profits, healthcare, and educational organizations. Additionally, through Felix Hern Speaks, I deliver engaging workshops and public speaking services to diverse clients. Let's work together to secure your organization's future in this AI-driven world. Contact me today to take the next step towards robust cybersecurity solutions.

About the Author

Dr. Felix Hernandez is a seasoned consultant with over twenty-five years of experience in Information Technology, Information Security, Project Management, and Business Development. Growing up in the South Bronx, NYC, he learned the value of hard work and determination at a young age, which has propelled him to success in his professional journey.

Dr. Hernandez owns and operates All American Technology Solutions Group, a leading consulting company providing IT services to small and medium-sized businesses. He also leads Strategic Sentinels, a boutique cybersecurity firm offering specialized services to non-profits, healthcare, and educational organizations. Additionally, through Felix Hern Speaks, he delivers engaging workshops and public speaking services to diverse clients.

He holds a Bachelor's degree in Information Systems Management from the New York Institute of Technology, a Master's degree in Information Management for Executives, and a Certificate of Advanced Studies in Information Security Management from Syracuse University. He also earned an Executive Education Certificate in Artificial Intelligence: Business Strategies and Applications from UC Berkeley and a Doctorate in Information Technology specializing in Information Assurance and Cybersecurity from Capella University.

Dr. Hernandez's industry credentials include CISSP (Certified Information Systems Security Professional), CISM (Certified Information Security Manager), CCSP (Certified Cloud Security Professional), CDPSE (Certified Data Privacy Solutions Engineer), CompTIA Security+, PMP (Project Management Professional), CEH (Certified Ethical Hacker), ITIL (Information Technology Infrastructure Library), and various certifications from Microsoft, Cisco, Citrix, and VMWare.

With over fifteen years of experience in training organizations and instructing students in higher education, Dr. Hernandez has served as a Professor of Ethical Hacking and Penetration Testing, Information

Systems and Security, and Enterprise Risk Management at several institutions across the United States.

In "Cybersecurity in the Age of Artificial Intelligence," Dr. Hernandez draws on his extensive background to provide valuable insights and practical strategies, helping readers understand and navigate the evolving landscape of cybersecurity in the AI era.

Contact Information:

Email: info@felixhernspeaks.com

LinkedIn: linkedin.com/in/felixhern/

Websites: www.felixhernspeaks.com,

www.aatsg.com,

www.strategicsentinels.com

References

BBC Worklife. (2023, December 19). Panic and possibility: What workers learned about AI in 2023. BBC. https://www.bbc.com/worklife/article/20231219-panic-and-possibility-what-workers-learned-about-ai-in-2023

Cloudflare. (n.d.). What is WannaCry ransomware? Cloudflare. https://www.cloudflare.com/learning/security/ransomware/wannacry-ransomware/?__cf_chl_rt_tk=JfBP_ycFzCw67_o3IhkocVPDU_B2YctVPwxd.Px2IuM-1721140218-0.0.1.1-5033

Conner, M. (2023, July 16). Generative AI phishing emails impact. TechRepublic. https://www.techrepublic.com/article/generative-ai-phishing-emails-impact/

Darktrace. (n.d.). Detect. Darktrace. https://darktrace.com/products/detect

Davis, J. (2023, May 10). Colonial Pipeline hack explained: Everything you need to know. TechTarget. https://www.techtarget.com/whatis/feature/Colonial-Pipeline-hack-explained-Everything-you-need-to-know#:~:text=The%20Colonial%20Pipeline%20was%20the,airlines%20along%20the%20East%20Coast

Gartner. (2021, July 21). Gartner predicts by 2025, cyber attackers will have weaponized operational technology environments to successfully harm or kill humans. Gartner. https://www.gartner.com/en/newsroom/press-releases/2021-07-21-gartner-predicts-by-2025-cyber-attackers-will-have-we

Security Magazine. (2020, April 20). Google blocks 18 million COVID-19 related scam emails each day. Security Magazine.

https://www.securitymagazine.com/articles/92188-google-blocks-18-million-covid-19-related-scam-emails-each-day#:~:text=Google%20Blocks%2018%20Million%20COVID%2D19%20Related%20Scam%20Emails%20Each%20Day,-April%2020%2C%202020&text=Google%20says%20that%20Gmail%20blocks,COVID%2Drelated%20daily%20spam%20messages

Sophos. (n.d.). AI in cybersecurity. Retrieved July 16, 2024, from https://www.sophos.com/en-us/cybersecurity-explained/ai-in-cybersecurity#:~:text=AI%20powered%20cybersecurity%20can%20monitor,common%20kinds%20of%20cyber%20attacks

Barracuda. (2024, March 22). How artificial intelligence is changing the threat landscape*. Retrieved July 16, 2024, from https://blog.barracuda.com/2024/03/22/how-artificial-intelligence-is-changing-the-threat-landscape

GovTech. (n.d.). Cybersecurity, deepfakes, and the human risk of AI fraud*. Retrieved July 16, 2024, from https://www.govtech.com/security/cybersecurity-deepfakes-and-the-human-risk-of-ai-fraud

Furman, J., & Rahwan, I. (2022). Artificial intelligence and the future of cybersecurity. AI Magazine, 43*(1), 56-67. https://doi.org/10.1080/08839514.2022.2037254

Superior Data Science. (n.d.). JP Morgan Coin: A case study of AI in finance. https://superiordatascience.com/jp-morgan-coin-a-case-study-of-ai-in-finance/#:~:text=Through%20its%20AI%2Ddriven%20Contract,minimizing%20human%20involvement%20post%2Ddeployment

Welch, C. (2018, August 13). DeepMind's AI can detect eye disease just as well as world-leading doctors. The Verge. https://www.theverge.com/2018/8/13/17670156/deepmind-ai-eye-disease-doctor-moorfields

Sophos. (n.d.). "AI in cybersecurity." Retrieved from https://www.sophos.com/en-us/cybersecurity-explained/ai-in-cybersecurity

Google. (n.d.). "AI-Based threat detection and response applications in threat". Retrieved from https://www.google.com/search?q=AI-Based+Threat+Detection+and+Response+Applications+in+threat&oq=AI-Based+Threat+Detection+and+Response+Applications+in+threat&aqs=chrome..69i57.1718j0j4&client=ms-android-transsion&sourceid=chrome-mobile&ie=UTF-8

Barracuda. (n.d.). "C-Ways security AI detection intelligence". Retrieved from https://blog.barracuda.c-ways-security-ai-detection-intelligence

SISA Information Security. (n.d.). "AI in cybersecurity: Incident response automation opportunities". Retrieved from https://www.sisainfosec.com/blogs/ai-in-cybersecurity-incident-response-automation-opportunities/

BlinkOps. (n.d.). "6 real-world applications of artificial intelligence (AI) in cybersecurity". Retrieved from https://www.blinkops.com/blog/6-real-world-applications-of-artificial-intelligence-ai-in-cybersecurity

Chapter 5National Institute of Standards and Technology. (2022, July 5). NIST announces first four quantum-resistant cryptographic algorithms. NIST.

https://www.nist.gov/news-events/news/2022/07/nist-announces-first-four-quantum-resistant-cryptographic-algorithms

George, J. (2023, September). When a quantum computer is able to break our encryption. RAND Corporation. https://www.rand.org/pubs/commentary/2023/09/when-a-quantum-computer-is-able-to-break-our-encryption.html

KPMG. (2024, March). Quantum and cybersecurity. KPMG. https://kpmg.com/xx/en/home/insights/2024/03/quantum-and-cybersecurity.html

Hacken. (n.d.). 51% attack. Hacken. https://hacken.io/discover/51-percent-attack/

IBM. (n.d.). Quantum computing. IBM. https://www.ibm.com/topics/quantum-computing

MSSP Alert. (2024). AI trends 2024: What the experts are saying. MSSP Alert. https://www.msspalert.com/news/ai-trends-2024-what-the-experts-are-saying

TechRepublic. (2023). IBM launches QRadar security suite. TechRepublic. https://www.techrepublic.com/article/ibm-launches-qradar-security-suite/

Channel Insider. (2024). Microsoft Security Copilot. Channel Insider. https://www.channelinsider.com/managed-services/microsoft-security-copilot/

Cybersecurity and Infrastructure Security Agency. (n.d.). NICE framework. National Initiative for Cybersecurity Careers and Studies. https://niccs.cisa.gov/workforce-development/nice-framework

European Union Agency for Cybersecurity. (n.d.). European cybersecurity skills framework. ENISA. https://www.enisa.europa.eu/topics/education/european-cybersecurity-skills-framework

UK Cyber Security Council. (n.d.). Cyber career framework. UK Cyber Security Council. https://www.ukcybersecuritycouncil.org.uk/careers-and-learning/cyber-career-framework/

\\\z

Note

Printed in Great Britain
by Amazon

49069868R00036